5 I

Win Being

You

Isha Cogborn

Founder of *Epiphany Institute and CoachIsha.com*

MW01229595

About The Author

Isha Cogborn believes that work shouldn't be a four-letter word. And that's what led her to launch Epiphany Institute, a professional development company that helps people shape purpose-driven careers and businesses.

Before becoming an entrepreneur, Isha worked to manage the brand of the largest chemical company in the world. From trade shows in Brazil to hosting live broadcasts from the United Nations, Isha excelled professionally, but suffered from severe work-related stress and chronic illness – a side effect of living a life disconnected from her purpose. When she was downsized at the height of the recession in 2009, Isha ordered new business cards *the very next day* and focused on rescuing people from unfulfilling careers.

Through coaching, training, keynotes and media appearances, Isha inspires women and men around the world to move beyond fear, uncertainty and confusion to walk confidently in their callings.

Check out her weekly tips to help you create the career of your dreams at **CoachIsha.com**.

.

5 Rules to Win Being You

Copyright © 2014 by Isha Cogborn

Scripture quotations noted AMP are from The Amplified Bible. Copyright© 1954,1958,1962,1964,1965,1987 by The Lockman Foundation. All rights reserved. Used by permission. (www.Lockman.org).

Scripture quotations noted MSG taken from THE MESSAGE. Copyright © 1993,1994, 1995, 1996, 2000, 2001, 2001. Used by permission of NavPress Publishing Group.

Previously released under the title: Five Rules to Win in the Business of Being You in 2012.

This book is available at quantity discounts for bulk purchases. For information, send an email to Info@CoachIsha.com.

To my mother, Gloria Ann Kling. Thank you for a lifetime of unconditional love and support.

Tag … you're it!

Contents

Everybody Loves the Underdog

"Everybody loves the underdog, and then they take an underdog and make him a hero and they hate him."
Fred Durst

What do Rocky, Titanic, and Snow White and the Seven Dwarfs all have in common? In addition to being a few of the most popular movies of all-time, they're classic underdog stories. You can't help but to feel good after watching the one who was counted out emerge victoriously. If you're watching a sporting event and don't have a favorite, who do you cheer for? The underdog, of course! Everybody loves a good underdog story…

Except when you're living it.

There's one underdog story that I've grown tired of, and it's the reason I wrote this book. It's the story that stars the talented individuals who get passed over time and time again for promotions. People running businesses that are on the verge of going under — not because they don't have a quality product or service – but because they can't seem to get the kind of "buzz" that their competitors generate.

What's Wrong with Being the Underdog?

Being the underdog is frustrating. How long will you remain committed to your employer if you don't feel like they see you as a valuable contributor? The role of the underdog is costly, too. Think about the cumulative value of the income you're losing on your job or in your business if you're not reaching your earnings potential.

But saddest of all, when you live life as the underdog, you're not making the impact on the world that you're capable of. No matter what you do for a living, you were put here for a purpose. If you're not fulfilling that purpose, your life is always going to feel like there's something missing. And those who would benefit from what you have to offer are missing out, too.

Why do we get comfortable playing the role of the underdog? Well, for some, it takes the pressure off. If people don't expect much from you, you won't disappoint them. Others have resigned themselves to believe mediocrity is their fate. They go through life believing there are two types of people – those who are successful and those who are people like them.

Believe it or not, there usually isn't bitterness towards the successful ones on the part of the underdogs. In fact, they take joy in rooting on others who used to be underdogs like them — the "regular" folks who caught a break. On the other hand, underdogs often loathe those whom they feel had it too easy or didn't pay their dues.

Why is Michael Jordan's athletic success so inspiring? Because he was cut from his high school basketball team. Why did the world fall in love with Britain's Got Talent phenom Susan Boyles? Or American Idol winner Taylor Hicks? Because they didn't *look* like typical superstars.

We love underdog stories so much because it gives us hope that one day, we too, might emerge victoriously. But if you want to go from underdog status to success story, there is one thing that must happen: **You must believe that you can win.**

But I Don't Feel Like a Winner

When you get comfortable in the role of perpetual underdog, it can be difficult to believe that winning is in your future. If you can't shift your thinking to believe that success is attainable, even if it does come, you'll chalk it up to a fluke.

Maybe you're confident in your professional abilities, but feel inadequate in other areas of your life. If you're not careful, this toxicity can permeate your career or business, too.

The World Boxing Council has 35 pages of rules to govern its fighters. When it comes to winning in the business of being you, the list could be just as long. What I've done in this book is identify five important principles — or rules — to guide you to professional success, whether you own a business, work for someone else, or both.

In case you didn't know, I'm a coach. I was driven down this path because in my years of speaking and training, I'd get so frustrated when someone would tell me how life-changing my message was, but if I ran into them six months later and asked them what they put into action, nothing had changed. I know I can't take ownership for the inactivity of others, but I also understand that it's easy to get caught up in the busyness of life and not apply the lessons we learn — no matter how impactful they may have been.

Throughout this book, I'm going to ask you to put what we've talked about to use right away. You may be tempted to skip ahead to the next chapter, but don't. You'll tell yourself that you'll come back to it later, but you won't. So make the commitment before you read another page of this book to complete the exercises that I've outlined for you. Many of the questions will force you to dig deep. It may not feel good, but you'll be glad you did.

chapter 1

The Fight of My Life

"It's not the size of the dog in the fight; it's the size of the fight in the dog."
Mark Twain

My senior year of high school, I was voted most likely to succeed. I wasn't the valedictorian; in fact, I graduated with a modest 2.9 grade point average. But sitting in that advanced placement English class with the smartest kids in the school, I still felt like I belonged.

The week after I arrived on the campus of Central Michigan University, I found myself in the school clinic for a pregnancy test. What would I do if the nurse said it was positive? How would I tell my parents? How would I finish school?

I was three hours away from home, and if I was expecting, the baby would be due during second semester's exam week. Labor and finals are not a good combination. I started thinking about all of the people who expected so

7

much from me who would now see me as a failure if I was pregnant.

The test was positive ... I was pregnant.

How could I be careless enough to get pregnant the week before I left for college? I had two choices: (1) hang my head in shame and live out the lowered expectations that most folks now had for me, or (2) put on my big-girl pants and figure out how to make this thing work. I chose the latter.

The plan was to take a semester off, move back in with my parents, and work full-time until the baby was born in May. I'd enroll in summer school at the community college in June and return to CMU full-time in August with the baby on my hip.

In May I gave birth to my son and as originally planned, I enrolled in summer classes, but had to drop them because I didn't have transportation. Instead of focusing on returning to college, I was trying to figure out if there was any future between me and my son's father. Before motherhood, I had once dreamed of national television audiences and being on stage in front of packed auditoriums, but now I was living in government-subsidized housing and selling cell phones and pagers for barely more than minimum wage. Worst of all, I was starting to accept that this would be my life for good.

The Turning Point

About one year after my son's birth, I was sitting at the cash register at work. The store was empty, and it had been a really slow day. Out of nowhere, in an almost audible voice I heard, "You weren't meant to be a regular person." I knew clearly that it was God speaking to me, and I knew exactly what it meant. The life I was living wasn't my destiny. Within a week, plans were in motion to return to college.

I was so excited to be back on campus. I felt alive for the first time in over a year. Taking a full load of classes, working as many as three part-time jobs at a time, and taking care of my son on my own wasn't easy. But living in poverty for the next thirty years wouldn't have been either. Three days after my son's fifth birthday, I earned my bachelor's degree — with a much higher grade point average than high school.

I've Arrived ... or Not

After graduation, I was hired by the largest chemical company in the world and moved to Lake Jackson, Texas. At only age 24, I was the employee communications manager for the company's largest site in the world. I had a wonderful manager and worked with some of the greatest people on the planet.

However, as great as things were, within a year, I couldn't help but to feel like I was supposed to be doing something else with my life. When I looked around the company, I didn't see anybody I wanted to be "when I grew up." I remembered the visions I had from childhood of being on the stage. I had studied broadcast journalism and although I ruled out a career in news, I still felt like I was supposed to do something in television. The path I was on looked nothing like what I dreamed my life would be. It was a far cry from sleeping on that mattress on the floor, but I was starting to feel dead again. So I begged God to show me what my purpose was.

Every now and then I'd get a puzzle piece, some small detail related to my future. As exciting as the revelations were, they were equally frustrating. It was like having random pieces of a huge jigsaw puzzle without seeing the picture on the box to know how they fit together.

After hiring a coach, I had more clarity about the future of my professional life than ever before, and it was so exciting! At that point, I had no idea how or when these things would happen, but the hope for what was possible was enough to sustain me. A few months earlier, I had taken a reassignment back to Michigan. I wasn't excited about the role, but I knew it was time for a change. One night I was up late working on a presentation for one of my project teams and I didn't feel well. I had never felt this type of pain. Within a couple of hours, I couldn't even stand up straight, so I drove myself to the emergency room. Little did I know, I wouldn't be finishing the presentation. In fact, I was on medical leave for the next four months.

The next few years were up and down. There were many times when I was ready to throw in the towel, but then I'd get a new role, a bonus, stock options, or an exciting assignment that would tide me over. I had stopped working with my coach after a multi-book contract forced her to stop serving one-on-one clients. Before long, the career dreams that I was so excited about barely even crossed my mind. Maybe I would be here until I retired. I still didn't have any aspirations in the company, so I decided to create my own role.

I thought about the things that I enjoyed, what I was really good at, and all of the knowledge I had gained having now held seven different roles in just as many years. What could I do that would bring value to the company that no one else could do? What problem could I confidently solve?

I drew up a job description along with the value proposition, sat down with the decision makers and my proposal was approved without objection.

Before I fully transitioned into my new assignment, my manager came into my office one morning and closed the door. I know it was either really good or really bad. But actually, it was neither. He told me that the newly-hired global communications and branding manager for one of our upstart business units had quit and they wanted me to replace her. The job was in Houston, Texas and would be a significant promotion. And by the way, I had about three days to make a decision. What would I do? Take the money, or move into the job I had created for myself?

I took the money.

It wasn't just about the money. When you're on a certain track — one that leads to major opportunities — it's an unwritten rule in most companies that you take every assignment offered to you. If you don't, you might not be on that track for long.

Almost Losing It

After six months, the job was wearing me out and my personal life was falling apart. My son who was 13 left me to live with his father in Phoenix, Arizona. The man I was casually dating got engaged to someone else. My cat even died! I was all alone, barely sleeping, and gaining a ton of weight. In the midst of traveling constantly and working as many as 70 hours a week, I also had to find time to sell my house in Michigan and buy a new one in Houston.

I was at a conference in Washington, D.C. for the 100th anniversary of a service organization I had been a part of since college. I should have been enjoying the historic celebration, but instead, I was sitting in the lobby of the J.W. Marriott Hotel looking up residential mental health facilities. I called my manager to tell her I couldn't do this anymore, but thank God, she wasn't in her office. I was in no position financially to quit, but I had reached my breaking point.

After a little sleep and lots of prayer, I made it back from the edge and returned home back to my normal routine.

We had three big trade shows planned for the business launch: Denver, Colorado; Rio de Janeiro, Brazil and Dubai, United Arab Emirates. At the last minute, the attendee list for Dubai was cut. The economy was tanking and a relocation ban bought me some time before making the move to Houston, which was a huge relief. I had accepted the job with the caveat that I would be able to work from Michigan one week a month to spend time with my son, who was originally planning to stay with his father there. When his dad decided to move to Phoenix, I knew all bets were off when it came down to my flexible work arrangement. Try explaining to your colleagues that you're actually working during your monthly trips to the Grand Canyon State.

The day after Halloween, which was the night I should have left for Dubai, I got a phone call from my mother.

My brother had been murdered.

In classic Isha fashion, I shifted to solution mode. I would pack up my clothes immediately and make the two-hour drive to my mother's house and begin making funeral arrangements on Monday. But I couldn't pack. I couldn't do anything but lay across my bed. I felt like the walls were closing in on me. I have the greatest friends in the world, and I knew they would be on my doorstep the moment they heard the news, but I just couldn't handle that right now. I didn't want to see or talk to anyone. I just wanted to wake up from this nightmare that had become my life.

After planning and canceling funeral arrangements in Michigan twice, we ended up flying to Los Angeles where my brother, Damion, lived. I got a call from a friend who was a leader in another department of the company where I worked. She warned me that layoff decisions were underway, and I needed to hurry back to work. But my job was the last thing on my mind. My brother had just been gunned down in the street on Halloween.

Exit Strategy

It took well over a week to bury my brother and by the time I got back to work, I was completely checked out. And I think everybody knew it. Damion didn't even live to see his 40th birthday. And deep down, I knew if I didn't make a career change, I wouldn't either.

The week after I returned, I got up one Saturday and went to a local diner alone to get my thoughts together. I knew I had to get out, but how? I went back to the plans I talked about with my coach four years prior. I looked at my finances and figured out exactly how much money I needed to be comfortable walking away from my job. Next, I scribbled out a plan to save more and earn more and figured out how long it would take to reach that number. Once again, my hope was restored.

Less than two weeks after I developed my exit strategy, there was an announcement that massive layoffs were coming. The first thing I did was calculate what I thought my severance package would be. You won't believe this, but it was the same number in my exit strategy!

On January 14, 2009, I was downsized. On January 15, 2009, I ordered new business cards and began the launch of my new company, Epiphany Institute.

Fight to Win

No matter where you grew up, how old you are, if you have six zeros in your bank account or just one, we've all had our share of challenges in life. Some have been self-imposed and others have been imposed upon us. Whatever you've been through, are currently going through, or may be getting ready to go through, this truth remains the same — you have options. You can decide to let your circumstances get the best of you, or you can adjust and keep moving forward.

Even when I felt like I was about to lose my mind, I began exercising the options that were available to me. Quitting certainly wouldn't have been a good option at the time, but it was still an option that I had the power to exercise. I was not a victim.

Don't allow yourself to feel like a victim. You still have power. Make adjustments and keep moving forward.

Time for Action

If any part of my story resonates with you, then it is time to get unstuck and take action. Let's start with reflecting on where you have been and where you are currently. I encourage you to write your answers in this book or in a journal you have dedicated to this process.

1. **In what areas of my business, career, or life have I allowed myself to become paralyzed?**

2. **What do I want to happen in these areas?**

3. **What options are available to me?**

4. Which options will most likely lead to my desired outcome?

5. What additional information do I need to move forward?

6. My plan and timeline for gathering this information and moving forward:

chapter 2

RULE No. 1: Pick the Right Fights

*"There are thousands and thousands of people out
there leading lives of quiet, screaming desperation, where
they work long, hard hours at jobs they hate to enable thing
to buy things they don't need to impress people
they don't like."*

Nigel Marsh

One of the greatest disappointments in life is to spend it
pursuing a goal only to realize that achieving it wasn't what
you truly wanted, that it didn't bring the fulfillment you
expected, or that you sacrificed too much to get there.

Pursuing the wrong goals is like a heavyweight boxer
fighting a lightweight — you may win, but it won't count.

When Nadia Brown started her career, her goal was to
climb the corporate ladder and make as much money as she
could.

"I wanted a two-story house, a black BMW, no husband, and no kids," she shared.

But somewhere along the way, her desires changed. For starters, she met a wonderful man and got married. And after a few years, she realized climbing the corporate ladder wasn't for her after all.

"I recall one of my older colleagues telling me, 'Nadia, this isn't for you. You need to start your own business.' I thought, 'Yeah right, I just need to find the right company!"

But company after company, position after position, Nadia was still frustrated.

"When I was laid off in 2010, it was becoming clear to me that the corporate lifestyle wasn't working for me, but I didn't know what I wanted to do," Nadia said.

"So I did what any level-headed person would do — I went back to work!"

But her hard-driving passion for her career had become a thing of the past.

"It wasn't a big deal for me to work 60 or 70 hours a week. That was just what I did. The day I came home and decided that I would work my 40 hours and not a minute more, I realized something had to change. I couldn't do it anymore. I wanted out."

Nadia devoted herself to prayer and journaling, asking God what He wanted her to do; what her purpose was. That was when Nadia and I started working together.

"You helped me put words to what I was feeling and make sense of it," Nadia told me.

We worked together to craft the vision for what became Doyenne Leadership Institute, a leadership development firm that helps women find their authentic leadership style and develop the confidence to excel.

"Like building a house, becoming an effective leader is a process," Nadia said. "At Doyenne, we're focused on building authentic female leaders one brick at a time. Brick houses can withstand the winds of change and storms they're bound to experience throughout their corporate careers. We help them to understand what comes with sitting in that executive's chair."

Nadia doesn't live in a two-story house and she drives a Toyota instead of a BMW, but her newfound career path has brought more joy than anything she could buy.

"Every day I get to wake up and do what I love and it's so exciting!" Nadia said. "I've gained a greater level of peace and confidence since I became an entrepreneur. I have more control over my schedule and have the freedom to make adjustments for my family when necessary."

Nadia's new career path has also brought about another unexpected change.

"I have a new circle of friends, because I've surrounded myself with other entrepreneurs. They're my support team," Nadia said.

Like Nadia, do you feel like what you want from your career has changed? If so, Nadia offers this advice: "Embrace it. It's easy to look at all you've invested into getting where you are today and feel like you'll let it go to waste if you change courses, but try not to think of it that way. It may also feel big and scary. Allow yourself to go through those emotions — don't dismiss them. But stay away from negative people! There will be people who will try to convince you to stay where you are. They may love you, but much of their input isn't about you; it's about their own discomfort."

Nadia's final piece of advice?

"Get a coach. Someone who can help you clarify what you want and what you need to do. When you think about leaving something certain for something fuzzy, it can be pretty scary. A good coach can help you develop the vision and the plan, and also hold your feet to the fire to actually achieve it."

Are you on the right path or are you still chasing a vision for your life that you've outgrown? Here are three questions to ask yourself about your professional goals:

Question No. 1: Why am I pursuing this goal?

Is it truly important to you or are you doing it because you feel like you "should"? If you have a formal performance management process at work, there may be goals that are dictated to you because of their impact on the bigger picture. However, I have also seen cases where unreasonable performance metrics are put in place in the spirit of continuous improvement, when time and energy could be redirected where it will be more beneficial.

If you haven't done so recently, take a moment to update the vision for your life. The lines between who we are and what we do are becoming increasingly blurred, so make sure the vision includes all areas of your life. Be sure your professional goals line up so that you're not wasting time and energy working on the wrong things.

When you look at your personal life, are you working to hit milestones like starting a family or making major purchases simply because you feel like you ought to have these things at this stage in your life? Don't make your future family miserable or go into unnecessary debt just to check a box. Focus on what you really want.

Question No. 2: What are the benefits of reaching this goal?

The answer to this question will be a great source of motivation to you on the days when you're ready to quit. When I was in college, working three part-time jobs and raising my son, I had to remind myself almost daily that earning my degree would allow me to provide him with a better quality of life than the path I was on previously.

Your answer can also help you to narrow your focus. One of the greatest threats to achieving your goals is having too many goals to begin with. If you find that you've bitten off more than you can chew, this simple question can be a handy tool to help you identify the most impactful efforts.

Question No. 3: What sacrifices might I need to make to achieve this goal? Do the benefits outweigh the sacrifices?

I can't think of too many things worth having that don't require sacrifice. When I decided to start my business, I knew I wasn't guaranteed a big monthly paycheck like I was used to in a corporate job. I moved into an apartment, cut off cable, and gave up my newer car for one that I could purchase outright instead of making a monthly payment. My car is old enough to legally drink, but it runs! We haven't taken a family vacation in a couple of years, and I can't go shopping every week like I had in times past.

I've made lots of sacrifices for entrepreneurship, but when I think about the satisfaction I get from waking up every day knowing with certainty that what I'm doing is making a difference in the lives of the people I work with and that I'm doing exactly what I was created to do, it's worth everything I've given up.

Nadia's greatest sacrifice was also a steady paycheck. "Even when I hated my job, I was happy at least two days a month — paydays!" she joked. "But the change has caused me to be more financially prudent — much to my husband's delight."

What might you need to sacrifice in order to reach each goal? If it's worth it, pursue it. If the cost is too high, perhaps your efforts should be postponed until things level out. Keep in mind: Delayed doesn't mean denied. Focus on doing what you can to minimize risks or disruptions so that you're able to enjoy the achievement of the goal, and more importantly, the manifestation of the full vision for your life.

Are you on the right path or are you still chasing visions for your life that you've outgrown?

Time for Action

1. What is the vision for my life?

2. How do the current goals that I'm pursuing line up to the vision?

3. Why am I pursuing these goals?

4. What are the benefits of reaching these goals?

5. What sacrifices might I need to make to achieve this goal? Do the benefits outweigh the sacrifices?

chapter 3

Is This REALLY What I Wanted to Be When I Grew Up?

It takes courage to grow up and become who you really are.
E.E. Cummings

Do you feel like a square peg in a round hole when it comes to your career? I know I did. And I felt guilty because I knew there were people who would have given their left thumb for my job. I didn't want to ever be accused of being ungrateful, but at the same time, I knew I didn't belong there. But until I figured out what it was that I did want to do, I felt trapped.

When I talk to people who are in professional situations they don't want to be in, they often tell me that they don't feel like they have better options. "If not this, what?" They will ask.

I have also witnessed people jump out of the frying pan into the fire saying yes to career or business opportunities they aren't interested in because of desperation.

I see a lot of this in the network marketing and direct sales industry. According to the Direct Selling Association, there were 15.6 million people involved in multi-level and direct marketing companies in the United States alone in 2011. For many, these business opportunities present a great opportunity to bring in a few extra hundred dollars a month for a vacation or to close the gap between earnings and rising expenses. But there are lots of others who sign up looking for their golden ticket out of the corporate rat race.

Here's a recipe for disaster ...

You sign up for a business selling products or services you're not really excited about, but because it's something that everyone needs, you're sure it will sell itself. But the products don't sell themselves. In fact, you're spending countless hours following up with prospective customers and business partners. When you realize you're not making money as quickly as you imagined you would, the excitement begins to wear off and now it feels like another job. Before long, you've given up on the business and are not any closer to the financial freedom you were seeking.

Please don't misunderstand me. I'm not against direct marketing businesses. However, I find it disappointing that people don't do a better job of finding business opportunities that are more closely aligned with their interests or ultimate goals. If you're considering entrepreneurial endeavors – especially if it's something you're going to do on top of a "real job," make sure you enjoy it. If you don't, the chances that you'll put in the effort necessary to be financially successful are nearly non-existent.

When I started my coaching practice, I was involved in a multi-level marketing company that provided affordable online and group coaching for women. It appealed to me because it allowed me to provide a very reasonably priced alternative for women who weren't financially ready to work with me one-on-one. But I quickly realized that substantial earnings in that business wouldn't come from getting new clients — it could only come from recruiting other successful representatives. I didn't enjoy recruiting, so I got out.

Just the same, many people move from job to job believing if they didn't work with such unreasonable people or if they could only make more money, their career problems would come to an end.

What if the problem isn't your company, your compensation or your colleagues? What if the problem is you?

Have you ever considered that maybe you are in the wrong field? That no matter how much money you make, your square peg will never be comfortable in that round hole? A different name on your paycheck won't change that. It can only be solved by figuring out what your purpose is.

I'm a firm believer that our lives are not some cosmic accident. I believe that you and I were both created by God to fulfill a specific purpose. And when we live out that purpose, we find true fulfillment and make a meaningful contribution to the lives of others.

How do you discover your purpose? Here are three things you can do to get on the right path:

1. **Consult the Manufacturer**
   If you want to know why you were created, why not ask the One who created you? Nadia talked about how prayer and journaling helped her to discover her purpose. You are a one-of-a-kind invention. Praying for insight about where your unique talents and skills will be best put to use is a worthwhile endeavor.

2. **Play the Detective**

   Your life is full of clues that connect to your purpose. Your path isn't as random as it may seem. In the "Time for Action" section at the end of this chapter, I'll guide you through a series of questions to help you identify a few of those clues.

3. **Be Patient with the Process**

   Discovering your purpose isn't an overnight pursuit. It could take months, or even years to figure it out. You may find that you'll get new puzzle pieces here and there and won't have a clue as to how they fit together. If you're the type of person who likes to have all the answers, you'll probably find this process frustrating. Get used to it, because learning to operate with a reasonable level of uncertainty is critical to living life beyond the status quo.

   Failing to discover your purpose is like having a valuable gift and never bothering to unwrap it. Make a commitment to yourself and the people who will benefit from what you're ultimately called to do that you'll see the process through — no matter how long it takes.

Learning to
operate with a
reasonable level of
uncertainty
is critical to
living life beyond
the status quo.

Time for Action

It's time to play the detective and identify some of the clues that may be pointing to your purpose. Be sure to provide three answers to each question so you have enough data to notice trends that will emerge.

Just Three Things

1. Three things I'm really good at:

2. Three things that make me different from many other people:

3. Three things I really enjoy doing:

4. Three specific ways I would enjoy helping others:

5. Three things I'd like to learn more about:

6. Three ways I would spend my time if I could do anything:

7. Three unfortunate things that have happened in my life:

8. Three of the happiest moments in my life:

9. Three things I want to do before I leave the earth:

10. Three times when I felt really smart or special:

Review your answers. You will likely see three themes emerge — common threads that show up in multiple responses. Write down the trends or themes you notice here:

chapter 4

The Tale of the TAPE

"Do not free a camel of the burden of his hump; you may be freeing him from being a camel."

G.K. Chesterton

Have you ever watched a boxing match? If so, you may have noticed that before the fight begins, there's a segment called "The Tale of the Tape." The commentators compare each boxer head-to-head looking at data points, such as their professional record, height, weight, age, and even the length of their arms. The statistics reveal each contender's unfair competitive advantage over the other.

If a fighter is ten years younger or their arms are three inches longer, those are unfair competitive advantages. I call them *unfair* because the fighters didn't have to work to gain the edge — it's just who they are.

When "Sugar" Shane Mosley fought Manny Pacquiao in 2011, Mosley dominated most categories of The Tale of the Tape. Yet there was one very important category where

"Pacman" held a clear advantage – his age. Eight years his junior, Pacquiao made Mosley look like a dinosaur in the ring.

When it comes to your professional capabilities, you may feel that you don't measure up to the people around you. Many of us have been wired this way since childhood. We lined up according to height and being the tallest or the shortest often made kids feel special. Awards were given to the best spellers and the fastest runners. If you weren't recognized as first place at something, you could easily start to believe that everyone else is better than you.

But all it takes is a single competitive advantage to make a world of difference. And even better, your *unfair* competitive advantage is already there — you simply need to discover it.

So what is *your* unfair competitive advantage? What attributes do you possess that can help you win by simply being who you already are? To figure that out, let's look at your Tale of the TAPE — talents, abilities, passions, and experiences.

Think about your last job interview. What did you do to stand out? Maybe put on your sharpest outfit? Possibly make sure your credentials were prominently featured on your resume? Is that really enough to separate you from the pack?

If you look around your industry, you may not have to look too far to find someone with an educational background comparable to yours. But you'd be hard pressed to find someone else with your TAPE — it's like your fingerprint. And when you learn to integrate this powerful formula into the work you do, you'll unlock the ability to deliver results and enjoy personal fulfillment like never before.

Talents

Let's start with your talents. What are you naturally gifted at that might not come so easily to other people? What activities put you into a zone where knocking it out of the park feels effortless?

Since I was a child, I've loved speaking. When other kids were crying because they had to do an Easter speech, I would cry because my speech wasn't the longest! Standing in front of an audience of 10,000 people is fun for me. Twisted, isn't it? Especially when so many people consider public speaking a fate worse than death.

Here's the thing about talents: There are some people that have what I call "showy talents:" Things everybody can easily recognize, like athletic or musical talent, high levels of creativity or extreme intelligence. But your talent doesn't have to be something that's going to get you on the cover of a magazine to be special.

It's often challenging to identify our talents because we think the things that come easy to us come easy to other people, too. I didn't realize my speaking talents were special until I started doing it competitively. But just because they don't give out national awards for your talent doesn't mean it isn't valuable. In fact, the only valuable talent is one that is put to use.

Maybe you're good at organizing things or working with children. Perhaps you're a wiz with numbers or have a knack for making complicated concepts easy for others to understand. What's *your* thing?

This is no time for modesty either. If you can't give yourself credit for the talents you possess, how can you ever expect someone else to do so?

Abilities

Now, let's move on to the A in your Tale of the TAPE, which stands for abilities. The difference between talents and abilities is that talents come naturally while abilities are things that you've learned how to be good at. This could be anything from technical certifications to being fluent in a foreign language.

In this formula, there's another important distinction to note when you're looking at your abilities: To be included in your TAPE, it should be your strength, not just something you *can* do. Out of necessity, I picked up ability in the area of graphic design. I'm able to do it better than many, but I wouldn't call it my strength. Someone who really knows what they're doing could do a much better job in a fraction of the time. Many of us have learned to be Jacks and Jills of all trades. But just because we know how to do something doesn't mean we do it well. For the purpose of this exercise, only focus on the things you do well.

Passions

What gets you really excited ... or really angry? What would you be willing to do for 40 hours a week without collecting a paycheck? What would make you write a letter to your congressman or protest in 10-degree weather? Where is your heart?

A few years ago I discovered that I'm passionate about helping people to find and live their purpose. Seeing people who are doing the thing they were put on this earth to do brings me amazing joy. And when people allow their talents to go to waste, it makes me very, very angry.

My brother, Damion, was a very talented musician before his death in 2008. His band Spade Ghetto Destruction inked a deal with a major record label back in 1994 and was on the cusp of breakout success. They even played at the birthday party for Francis Ford Coppola's daughter. Damion experienced a high like no other when he was performing. But because of bad habits and decisions, success never came at the level they were capable of achieving. They often talked about getting the band back together, but it didn't happen.

I have to admit, when my brother died, I was angry with him. I felt like he wasn't a good steward over the talents and opportunities he had been given. But I quickly realized that I hadn't been either.

Before getting laid off, most of my talents were dormant. My speaking engagements were few and far between. And although I had begun the process to become a certified life and business coach, I hadn't been investing any time or effort in laying the groundwork to launch my practice. I was too tired. Too busy. Damion's death was the wakeup call I needed to focus on living my purpose. And I quickly realized how passionate I was about helping others to do the same.

Experiences

Perhaps the most valuable component of your TAPE is your experiences. What has happened in your life — good or bad — to shape you into the person you are today?

We all see the world through a different lens based on our experiences. If you grew up in an affluent neighborhood, you may have seen a police car driving down the street as reassurance that the people and things you treasure are protected. However, if you grew up in a neighborhood where tensions between residents and cops run high, that same police car may have been viewed as a threat. Neither perspective is right or wrong; they are simply shaped by the lens of personal experiences.

As I mentioned earlier, we've all had our share of challenges in life. Ironically, your greatest challenges may serve as a source for your greatest unfair competitive advantage. Experiencing poverty as a young single mother eliminated fears around money that many folks who transition from employment to entrepreneurship face. I knew what it felt like to not have a dime to my name — literally. And it didn't kill me. Now, if I encounter financial crisis, it doesn't scare me. I recognize it as a temporary situation that I'll overcome. And I get to work!

I believe the *Holy Bible* is the best business and personal development book ever written. Romans 8:28 states, "And we know all things work together for good to them that love God, to them who are the called according to His purpose." This is great news because it tells us that when we're fulfilling the purpose that God created us for, everything will work together for our good. All of the pieces — good, bad, and ugly — are masterfully orchestrated together to create the symphony of our lives when we're walking in our purpose. That's another good reason to commit to discovering your purpose.

In order to get the most out of this component of your TAPE, you have to be willing to acknowledge some of the not-so-pleasant things that have happened in your life if they've had a profound impact on the person you are today. You'll be amazed at how certain life experiences will allow you to connect with a customer in a way that no one else can, solve a problem in an innovative way, or just remind you how strong and capable you are. Don't hide from your experiences. They just may be the key to your next level of success.

Other people may have the same education that you have, own the same power suit that you wear to your interviews, and have studied all of the "right answers" to every question a hiring manager could possibly ask. But what are the odds that any of the other 7 billion people on the planet can match your TAPE identically? They may share the same talents, but do they see the world the way you do based on the life you've lived? Once you've discovered your TAPE, then you can focus on how to put it to work for you. We'll talk about that in the next chapter.

All it takes is a single competitive advantage to make a world of difference.

Time for Action

Begin to discover your Tale of the TAPE by thoughtfully answering the following questions:

Talents:
What are you naturally gifted at? What comes easy for you to do? What types of tasks or projects do others usually ask you to help with or to lead?

Abilities:
What have you learned to be good at?

Passions:
What gets you really excited or upset? What causes you to spring effortlessly into action?

Experiences:
What has happened in your life — good or bad — that has shaped the way you see the world or relate to people?

chapter 5

Your TAPE in Action

"Problems are only opportunities in work clothes."

Henri Kaiser

If you want to unleash your unfair competitive advantage through your TAPE, here's the question to which you must find the answer:

Who am I uniquely gifted to serve and what problem can I confidently help them solve?

Knowing and being able to articulate the answer to this question can be the difference between business success and bankruptcy. It can take you from being seen as just another cog in the wheel at work to being recognized as an indispensable contributor.

When I first started Epiphany Institute, I was a generic life coach. If you had a problem, I could help you solve it. Before long, I realized there were certain clients that I

47

absolutely loved working with: people who wanted to leave their corporate careers and start businesses aligned to their purpose. I've been able to deliver extraordinary results for these clients, because I lived it. The stress, illness, and frustration of feeling stuck in one career when I really wanted to do something else paid off by uniquely equipping me to help others get on a path that leads to greater fulfillment.

What if I had been married and our household finances allowed me to quit at the first sign of frustration in my corporate career? I may have still had a successful coaching practice, but my ability to understand my clients as deeply as I do today wouldn't be there. As I listen to their pain, it takes me back to the days when I secretly wished my illness would return just so I could get away from the stress of my job. My clients know I "get it," and that's why they choose me over other coaches.

There are two parts to the important question you must answer: (1) the "who" and (2) the problem. Here's what it looked like for Robert:

When Robert looked at his Just Three Things and TAPE, he realized he had a strong passion for animals. In his first role out of college, he worked as a project manager for an events management company that specialized in planning charity events for its high-profile clients. Several years had passed since he moved on to another company, but he still had lots of contacts and the processes had become second nature to him.

Robert contacted the director of the animal shelter where he volunteered occasionally and offered to arrange a fundraising event for the organization. Because they didn't have the funds to pay him, he drew up a contract stating that his compensation would be 15 percent of any profits brought in after expenses. If the event made no money, he made no money.

He pulled out his rolodex and called in favors from a number of his friends who had goods and services that could be donated to the fundraiser, which kept expenses low. He also enlisted the help of his sister, who was looking to build up her portfolio to apply for a role in her company's marketing department.

The event was a huge success resulting in thousands of dollars raised for the animal shelter, a nice paycheck for Robert, and phone calls from the nonprofit's branches in other cities who wanted to work with him to duplicate the effort.

Just like Robert, your experiences have likely provided you with a valuable skill set. Do your research and figure out how you can apply the TAPE to fix a problem related to your passions.

But here's a caveat: It must be a problem that people see as critical enough to solve. You might have the answer to keeping sugar packets perfectly straight in a serving dish, but will that lead to a substantial payday?

How many times have you seen a co-worker frustrated because their great idea wasn't supported by management? It doesn't mean what they wanted to work on wasn't important; it just wasn't a priority to the organization. Your charge is to use your TAPE to solve a priority problem. To the animal shelter, a lack of funds was a priority problem. Robert was able to use his TAPE to help them raise money without spending a lot of money to do it.

The Shift

A very important and exciting trend is taking place in the global economy. We're shifting from a labor-based market to an information and knowledge economy. People are willing to pay for solutions and they're more willing to try nontraditional methods to get their problems solved. This creates even greater opportunities for you to find a bigger market when it comes to the problem you confidently solve.

Here are three questions to ask yourself as you look to answer that very important question: Who am I uniquely gifted to serve and what problem can I confidently help them solve?

Question No. 1: Is this problem big enough that an organization or individuals will pay me to solve it?

Think about the organizations or individuals that you currently know with this need. Are there others you haven't thought of who have similar characteristics that would make them a good target market for you? If you're looking at a problem within the company you work for, are there other departments or divisions with similar issues?

Question No. 2: Does it recur, or are there enough people with this problem that I can create a sustainable income?

Don't box yourself in by your immediate geographic area. Technology is making it easier to bring your solution to broader audiences. When I launched my business, I made a conscious decision to work with my clients by phone so that I could serve people around the world and could travel anywhere and still be able to work.

Question No. 3: Can I package my solution into a product, service, or permanent role?

Your success is heavily dependent on making it easy for people to access your solution. On the job, it may be a matter of creating definitive work processes that others can follow. If you're in business, how will you let your customers know exactly what they're getting from you and what they'll pay for it? Does it make sense to create different levels of your offering so people can opt-in based on their specific level of need or what they want to invest in solving the problem? In essence, can you create a Ford Fiesta, Taurus, and Lincoln Town Car option?

Think about how the people you serve want to receive your solution. Will you do the work for them or give them the tools to do it themselves? Is it an off-the-shelf product, a training class or both? Allow yourself to think creatively. Traditional consulting isn't the only way to make money with your expertise. Look at what others are doing in similar and completely different industries and think about how these models could apply to the problem you solve and the people you serve.

Time for Action

Provide detailed answers to the following questions. For your audiences, be very specific. Be sure to refer to the responses in your Just Three Things and Tale of the TAPE exercises.

1. **Who does your TAPE uniquely equip you to serve?**

2. **What problem does your TAPE equip you to confidently solve for these audiences?**

3. **How specifically does your TAPE allow you to meet your audience's needs?**

4. Why is this need a priority to those who would pay you to fix it?

5. How could you generate recurring income by solving this problem?

6. If you were to package your solution as a product, what would it look like?

chapter 6

RULE No. 2: Don't Be Intimidated by Your Opponents

"When there is no enemy within, the enemies outside cannot hurt you."
African Proverb

One of the first times I taught the principles around unleashing your unfair competitive advantage, I had a visibly shaken woman from my audience come up to me on a break.

"Isha, I agree with what you're saying, but can't you find a nicer way to put it? Why does it have to be unfair? And why do we have to compete?" she asked.

That was a very valid question. For lots of folks, especially women, the word competition is synonymous with a "fight-to-the-death" battle that brings out the worst in everyone. But it doesn't have to be that way.

Competition is a part of life, but it doesn't have to turn you into someone your mother would be ashamed of. In fact, competition keeps us on top of our game. When there's no competition in an industry, innovation is almost non-existent, prices skyrocket, quality suffers, and customers are taken for granted. Knowing the people we serve have options ought to keep us focused on giving our best at all times.

Have you ever gone to a conference or networking event and met someone who was extremely accomplished? Instead of getting jealous or insecure, allow it to light a fire under you!

However, be careful to use others only as a benchmark, not a standard. Contentment in simply being a step ahead of others may allow you to get comfortable living beneath your true potential.

Please remember this: Your competitor doesn't have to be your enemy. I've seen the culture of organizations turn toxic as employees began to see their colleagues as an obstacle standing in the way of their professional goals. They take advantage of every opportunity to throw their co-workers under the bus or refuse to take on any assignment that won't end with accolades.

If a role or promotion belongs to you, no one can take it from you, but you can give it away by letting one of your internal — not external — opponents win. What are these internal opponents? Be mindful of these five:

1. Lack of Confidence
2. Fear of Failure
3. Fear of Success
4. Lack of Knowledge
5. Laziness and Procrastination

Far too often, it's our own attitudes, beliefs, habits, and behaviors that derail our opportunities to enjoy career or business success — not the actions of someone else. Over the next few chapters, we'll take a quick look at these five internal opponents and outline strategies to keep them on the ropes and possibly knocked out.

Competition
is a part of life,
but it doesn't have
to turn you into
someone your
mother would be
ashamed of.

chapter 7

The Confidence to Succeed

"Whatever we believe about ourselves and our ability comes true for us."

Susan L. Taylor

Hey Isha,

I just wanted to drop a note to say thank you again. Since our last meeting, I've been writing every day and even began querying websites/publications. Well, today I found out that one of the articles I submitted will be published tomorrow! After my initial shock, the first thing I thought to do was to thank you.

I've wanted to do this for years, but didn't quite have the courage to even try. I listened to people quote statistics and tell me how difficult it is to find work and earn a decent living. But there was something about the way you said 'you are a writer' in our last conversation that really made me believe it. You also told me my

59

writing was going to help others heal but nobody could be healed if I was too afraid to write. If not for that phone call, I still would not be writing.

So ....THANK YOU, THANK YOU, THANK YOU! You are an amazing woman and coach and I'm proud to know you. Keep doing what you're doing because you are really making a difference!

Tracy

When I initially connected with Tracy Jolly, she was struggling with how to make her dreams of becoming a professional writer come true. What you just read was the outcome of a 60-minute strategy session we had to help her get on track.

In her case, it wasn't figuring out how to do it. She understood the freelance writing industry. It was a matter of confidence. Tracy needed to see herself as a writer — not just as someone who can write. Today, she's inspiring and empowering women around the world to live bigger and better lives as the editor of the award-winning blog, *Losing My Mind, Finding My Voice.*

There are some people who just ooze confidence. It's like they're born with it. When they walk into a room, you can't help but to notice them. Even when they don't know the answer or make mistakes, it doesn't seem to shake them.

What if you aren't born with that kind of confidence? Just like a muscle, you can build it.

Three Ways to Build Your Confidence

1. **Knowledge**
   When you know your stuff, you're more confident. Think about it. When we're feeling uncertain about our professional future, what's the first thing we often consider? Earning a new degree or certification!

Invest the time, energy and resources into building your expertise. Consider joining professional organizations or mastermind groups. Stay current on new trends taking place in your industry. If you're considering a degree or costly certification that isn't absolutely critical to advancing professionally or improving your business, make sure you count the cost by taking your goals through the process outlined in Chapter Two.

One of the best ways to gain knowledge is through experience. Look for opportunities to volunteer your time or services in exchange for a chance to gain new capabilities.

2. Results

Having concrete results to stand on is the best way for others to build confidence in your abilities. For years, I had been procrastinating about gathering testimonials from my clients. I knew how important it was to provide social proof to those who were thinking about working with me, I just hadn't gotten around to it. As soon as I did, I saw the number of people signing on to work with me increase exponentially.

Take the time to assemble your track record. What results have you been instrumental in achieving for your company or clients in your current and previous roles? Even if they don't directly relate to the work you're doing now, look for ways to demonstrate how the effort or skills used to deliver previous results will allow you to add value in your new role.

3. Faith

How do you manage to have confidence in yourself when you don't have the knowledge, experience, or track record to prepare you for the task ahead of you?

That's when it's time to rely on a little divine intervention.

I'm reminded of the story of Gideon from the Bible (Judges 6-8). During a period when the Israelites were under the domination of the Midianites, Gideon, the weakest member of the weakest tribe, was commissioned by God to save His people from their oppressors. And if that wasn't a big enough challenge, God told him to go to battle against an army so large it was like trying to count the grains of sand on the seashore. The size of Gideon's army? A meager 300. It had been much larger, but God intentionally pruned it so that it would be clear to everyone that they were victorious, not because of their size or might, but only because He was with them.

You may find yourself in a fight that you know you can't possibly win with your capabilities alone. Maybe God is simply using it as an opportunity to show you what's possible when you learn to depend on Him?

Needless to say, Gideon's army was victorious. And you can be, too. Trade your fear in for faith and be confident in God's ability to do great things through you.

Time for Action

1. What one action can you start in the next 60 days to narrow a knowledge gap that's impacting your confidence?

2. What results have you helped to deliver in your current or previous roles?

3. How do these accomplishments support your ability to deliver value in your current or desired role?

4. In what areas do you need to release your fears and insecurities and rely on God?

chapter 8

Conquering the "F" Word

I've missed more than 9000 shots in my career. I've lost almost 300 games. Twenty six times, I've been trusted to take the game winning shot and missed. I've failed over and over and over again in my life. And that is why I succeed.

Michael Jordan

I wrote this book under extreme conditions. I had about a month from creating the outline to having the final copy in my hand from the printer. On top of it, I had multiple speaking engagements, started two new coaching groups on top of my normal client load and was traveling for two out of those four weeks.

Knowing all that I had going on, a dear friend of mine was absolutely mortified that I had committed to finishing this book so fast. But at the same time, I had two unfinished books on my hard drive that I failed to complete when I had plenty of time to work on them. I jumped out and made a commitment to a client to finish the book in time for their event, because I knew the attendees could really benefit from it. The information I had to share to could change the course of their early careers, so I had to get busy.

Without coming right out and saying it, my friend really wanted to ask, "What if your book is a failure?"

Failure: The ultimate F word. It's nasty enough to keep many from ever even taking a step toward making their professional dreams come true. I wonder how many books were never written, inventions never created, businesses never launched, and problems never solved because of the fear of failure.

The United States, in particular, has created a culture where missing the mark evokes fear in the heart of most people. What happened in elementary school when you were wrong? Big red mark. What about when you gave the right answer? Gold star! Every day children sit mortified in classrooms around the country afraid that they'll be called on and won't have the right answer.

This dangerous trend continues into adulthood as people sit in meetings with amazingly innovative ideas, but too afraid to speak up because their suggestion may not be well-received. What would happen if scientists halted their research whenever the first hypothesis didn't prove to be true? If companies threw in the towel whenever a product launch wasn't a blockbuster success?

Overcoming the fear of failure requires a process of unraveling these toxic thoughts. When I decided it was time to become a full-time entrepreneur, there were plenty of people with plenty of reasons why it wasn't prudent. We were experiencing a nasty recession in the U.S., and companies and individuals didn't have as much discretionary income for things like coaching and training. Here's the conversation I had with myself:

Q: What are your afraid of?
A: If my business doesn't take off soon enough, I could lose my house.

Q: Then what?
A: I'd have to move into an apartment and wait a few years to restore my credit before buying another home — or be successful enough that I can pay cash for the next one.

Q: What else could happen if you fail?
A: I'll have to figure out what I did wrong and start over, and possibly get a job until I build my financial reserves back up.

Q: Then what?

A: I could lose my savings, which would force me to be very conservative with my spending so that I can deal with any emergencies that arise.

Q: Are you capable of doing that?

A: Yes.

Q: What's the best thing that could happen if your business succeeds?

A: I will be in a position to help countless people around the world make their professional dreams come true. They'll make an impact on the world as they live their purpose, creating an immeasurably positive impact.

Q: What else could happen?

A: I could experience the satisfaction that comes from doing work I enjoy that utilizes my TAPE. I won't be sick and stressed out every day because of my work.

Q: Then what?

A: I'll be compensated well for what I do and be able to build a legacy for generations to come.

Q: Does what you stand to gain outweigh what you stand to lose?

A: Absolutely!

You know what? I did lose my house after I decided to move from Michigan to Arizona and couldn't maintain expenses in two locations while waiting for it to sell. And just as outlined above, I moved into an apartment. My worst fear was realized, but it wasn't the end of the world. If I had to do it over again knowing what the outcome would be, I would have still made the same choice.

Staying focused on what you have to gain takes the sting out of a temporary setback. And all setbacks are temporary as long as you don't quit.

Time for Action

1. When it comes down to the bottom line of going after what you *really* want, what's the worst that could happen if you fail?

2. If this fear is realized, what consequences would you suffer?

3. What would you have to do to recover?

4. What is the best thing that could happen if you're successful?

5. What benefits would you enjoy?

6. Does what you stand to gain outweigh what you could possibly lose?

chapter 9

Can I Really Handle Success?

*"The thing that makes you exceptional, if you are at all,
is inevitably that which must also make you lonely."*
Lorraine Hansberry

While the fear of failure never really rattled me, the fear of success did — and sometimes still does.

How do you know if you're afraid of success? Here are a few indicators:

- You know exactly what you need to do in order to be successful, but you're still not doing it.

- You're concerned that you may not be able to manage the expectations others will have of you as you reach higher levels.

- The thought of having to "let people in" to your life is unnerving.

- You're afraid that people will think you've changed if you don't have as much time for them or are no longer interested in the things you used to do.

- You're concerned about being able to trust the motives of people around you. Do they really care about you, or just what you can do for them?

My biggest fear has been how my success will change the people around me. And as much as we may like to believe that success will not change us, it will. If you're going to be successful as an executive in the company, you can't continue to think and function the same way you did as an entry-level employee. But there will be people around you who will want you to continue to be who you were when you started out.

When you're living on purpose doing what it is you were created to do, your priorities change. There's a sense of urgency around your efforts because you understand the impact your work has on those you serve. It doesn't mean you can't relax and enjoy social activities occasionally, but your life will be much more regimented than those who are not living on purpose.

As I write this, it's 5 a.m. and I haven't yet been to sleep. I've been working for eighteen straight hours. On top of it, I flew into my hometown in Michigan from Phoenix several days ago and have yet to see my friends and extended family because I've been focused completely on finishing this book.

Some would say, "You only live once ... enjoy your time at home." But people who understand the urgency of purpose don't even question my actions.

I had a dear friend jokingly say to me, "Am I going to have to start making an appointment with your assistant to talk to you on the phone?" It hurt my feelings, because deep down, I know that day may be coming. And it's a little scary.

Success can be a lonely place. And when your success is accompanied by notoriety or financial abundance, using discernment in your business and personal relationships is more and more critical.

So how do you overcome a fear of success? I'm not going to give you a five-step formula or ten questions to answer. It all comes down to one simple action — *choose success.*

You must decide that your commitment to the impact you've been called to make in the world is greater than the discomfort you'll experience as your life and the people around you change.

Will you really be able to live with the "what ifs" you're bound to face if you continue to function beneath your potential? Can you handle the frustration of looking at other successful people, knowing that you're smarter or more talented, and that the only reason you're not where they are is because you gave in to fear? Are you willing to settle for a second-class version of your life?

You have a choice to make. Choose wisely.

You must decide that
YOUR COMMITMENT
to the impact you've
been called to make
in the world is
**GREATER THAN THE
DISCOMFORT**
you'll experience as your
life and the people around
you change.

Time for Action

If you have decided to choose success, complete the pledge below.

I, _____

declare on the _____ day of _____

in the year of _____, **I choose success**.

_____

Signature

chapter 10

When You Don't Know What You Don't Know

"My people are destroyed for lack of knowledge ..."
Hosea 4:6

According to Google, information searches on its site surpassed an average 4.7 billion each month in 2011. The website WorldWideWebSize.com estimates that there are at least 9.42 billion pages of information indexed online. With the push of a button on your smart phone, you can locate a source for almost anything that you want to know within minutes. Yet, many people never even take the first step toward their professional dreams, because they don't know what to do.

Every week, I discover new tools or processes to function more effectively in my business. I have also made my share of mistakes because of things that I just didn't know. It's one thing when you don't know what you don't know. But it's unacceptable when we know exactly what information we need to move forward, yet fail to seek it out.

In addition to online searches, here are five tips to help you gather the intelligence you need to succeed:

1. Talk to others who have already done what you want to do. Prepare a list of questions in advance and be respectful of their time. If the person you're approaching shares the knowledge you're asking for as part of their business, offer to pay them. Asking a consultant if you can "pick their brain" over lunch is like buying a surgeon a cup of coffee to remove your gallstones. Make an effort to connect with at least one new person each month.

2. Find out what publications and websites successful people in your industry read, what groups they belong to, and who they look to as role models and mentors. If you don't know them personally, look at who they follow on Twitter or what Facebook pages they like.

3. When you join professional organizations or networking groups, don't just hide out, build

relationships and consider volunteering in a formal capacity if your schedule allows.

4. Find online groups where information related to your efforts is routinely shared. In 2011, I started a Facebook group called *... **But I Don't Want a REAL Job!*** for folks who have or want to start their own businesses. People from around the world convene in the group when their schedule permits, sharing tips, asking questions, and building their professional network. Do searches on LinkedIn, Facebook, or other social networking sites for a grout that will meet your needs.

5. Set aside a specific time each week for professional development. Trying to take in too much at a time can lead to analysis paralysis — questioning whether or not what you're doing is correct to the point you don't do anything.

Time for Action

Use the outline below to create your knowledge-building action plan.

Potential Experts to Interview:

Organizations to Research:

Websites/Publications to Read:

Online Groups to Engage In:

People to Follow Online:

chapter 11

Why it Can't Wait

You lazy fool, look at an ant. Watch it closely; let it teach you a thing or two. Nobody has to tell it what to do. All summer it stores up food; at harvest it stockpiles provisions. So how long are you going to laze around doing nothing? How long before you get out of bed? A nap here, a nap there, a day off here, a day off there, sit back, take it easy—do you know what comes next? Just this: You can look forward to a dirt-poor life, poverty your permanent houseguest!

Proverbs 6:6-11 (MSG)

Laziness and procrastination is a very powerful opponent. I think I'll write this chapter later.

Four Reasons Why We Procrastinate

Overwhelm. When you feel like there's too much to do and you don't know where to begin, a common reaction is to do nothing. Instead, break down the task or goal into small chunks that don't scare you – no matter how large or how long you feel it will take to accomplish it. Doing one small thing each day will get you further than doing nothing. Find ways to create a work process such as a checklist or spreadsheet that will allow you to chart your progress and give others a tool to hold you accountable.

Perfectionism. While excellence is attainable, perfection usually isn't. Don't allow yourself to get trapped in analysis paralysis – planning and reviewing continuously instead of pulling the trigger. Remember this: Done is better than perfect.

Pain. Completing a task we dislike may be painful, but the guilt of unfinished work hanging over your head hurts even more. Put yourself out of your misery and get it done!

Laziness. There are times when you'd just rather be doing something else...or nothing at all. Making time for leisure and relaxation are great, but not at the expense of your purpose.

chapter 12

RULE No. 3: Get the Right People in Your Corner

Where no counsel is, the people fall: but in the multitude of counselors there is safety.
Proverbs 11:14

Whether they've intentionally assembled them or not, you'll find that just about every successful person has a Personal Advisory Board. Who are these people? They're the ones you can trust to help you figure things out when it comes to your career or business.

I'm sure you've found that most people are more than willing to give you advice — whether they're qualified to or not. Receiving counsel from the right sources can have a tremendous impact on the success, so be careful who you listen to.

As you assemble your Personal Advisory Board, look to fill these critical roles:

Mentor

A good mentor is someone who is experienced and accomplished, and is invested in seeing you succeed. You may have more than one mentor to address different areas of your career or business.

If you don't have people around you who could fill this role, find a formal mentoring program through a professional or civic organization. If you're starting a business, connect with SCORE or the small business development office at the closest college or university. Collaborative and co-working spaces are popping up across the country each with its own unique structure and culture. A Google search will let you know what resources are available in your area or online.

Don't take your mentors for granted. Always look for ways to show your appreciation for the role they play in your life.

Cheerleader

When you're having a horrible day, who can you always count on to make your feel better? Who is that person who believes in you more than you believe in yourself? The person you can count on to support your efforts without judgment? If you don't have one, find one soon.

86

My cheerleader is my friend Kim. We've been friends since my first day on campus at Central Michigan University. And even though she didn't know what was going on, I even recruited her to go to the clinic with me when I took my pregnancy test.

Kim drove almost three hours to surprise me for my first speaking engagement after starting Epiphany Institute. She prays for me regularly. And I know beyond a shadow of a doubt, she'll be in my corner through thick and thin.

Challenger

How hard would a boxer train if they knew they had no challenger to face once they stepped into the ring? Although you may not enjoy your chats with this person as much as your cheerleader, the challenger plays one of the most critical roles in your professional development. This is the person who asks the tough questions and keeps you grounded.

My challenger is my friend Jarod. He's a lawyer; he's very left-brained and extremely risk-adverse. He was the one that questioned my ability to write this book in such a short period of time.

But what I love most about Jarod is that although I scare him with my hail-Mary business plans, he finds a way to voice his concern without being negative. This is the most critical characteristic that you must look for in your challenger. Someone who is negative instead of constructive will demoralize you.

If you have a more conservative personality, your ideal challenger may be someone who will push you to do more and dream bigger.

Confidante/Prayer Partner

A confidante or prayer partner plays a very critical role in your sanity. This is the individual that you can trust with everything — no matter how ugly it may be. Much like your cheerleader (and this may be the same person as your cheerleader), you don't have to concern yourself with being judged by your confidante.

It's one thing to have someone who will sympathize with you when you're in a bind. But how much more powerful is it to have someone who will pray for you?

Your Personal Advisory Board will be of no use to you if you don't learn to ask for help when you need it or if you feel like you already know everything. Be open to receiving counsel and being challenged on even your best ideas.

You're going to make mistakes. Big ones. But having a solid Personal Advisory Board in place can help you minimize the frequency and impact of errors by benefiting from the wisdom and experience of your mentor, having a challenger who will help you think things through before you act, a confidante to share your fears and blunders with, and a cheerleader to motivate you to stay in the fight.

Time for Action

It's time to assemble your Personal Advisory Board to increase your odds of professional success.

My Mentor:

My Cheerleader:

My Challenger:

My Confidante/Prayer Partner:

chapter 13

RULE No. 4: Commit to Your Training Plan

I hated every minute of training, but I said, 'Don't quit. Suffer now and live the rest of your life as a champion.'
Muhammad Ali

Boxing is widely regarded as one of the most physically and mentally demanding sports in the world. When preparing for a fight, athletes follow a carefully crafted regimen to give them the best shot at winning.

What will it take for you to win? Where do you need to devote consistent effort to create a professional life that allows you to fulfill your purpose and share the best of yourself with the world?

Size Up Your Opponent
A boxer's strategy changes depending on who they're fighting. Take a look at the five internal opponents we talked about earlier – lack of confidence, fear of failure,

fear of success, lack of knowledge and laziness and procrastination. Which one(s) do you need to knock out in order to win? This isn't about quick fixes either. Identify and address the root of the issue so that you're not just winning a round here or there; win the fight.

Good boxers also develop the ability of keeping their emotions under control. Well, most of them. You may remember that incident where a certain boxer bit off his opponent's ear? That would be an example of what *not* to do!

There may be times when you don't *feel* qualified for the assignment you've been called to take on. You may *feel* like lying on the couch in front of the television instead of putting in work on your entrepreneurial pursuits after a full day of work at your "real job". You may *feel* like the obstacles you're facing are too great to overcome. Don't let your feelings get the best of you. Take control!

A good way to do this is to create affirmations or spiritual declarations that remind you who you are and what you're going to do. Notice I didn't say what you're *trying* to do. Write them out and recite them aloud every day. Before long, those renegade thoughts and emotions will be subjected to the truth and your actions will line up.

Address Your Deficiencies

Every fighter has an area of weakness. The key to winning the match is to make sure your strengths overpower your weaknesses.

No one expects you to be perfect. However, allowing crucial weaknesses to go unaddressed can sabotage everything you're working so hard to gain. A deficiency could be something that you're just not good at. Or it could be a personality trait that has hindered you in the past. If it has the potential of derailing your success, don't ignore it.

Here's an example from my son's favorite sport basketball. Retired National Basketball Association star Shaquille O'Neal was one of the heaviest athletes to ever play in the league at 325 pounds. However, he used his size and strength as an advantage to overpower opponents both offensively and defensively.

He amassed impressive stats over his 18-year career, but free-throw shooting wasn't one of them. At his lowest point, Shaq shot a disappointing 38 percent from the line, and in 2000, during a game, against the Seattle Supersonics, he missed all 11 of his attempts. He did manage to set a record with that one!

Opponents wasted no time exploiting his weakness with a strategy known as "Hack-a-Shaq." If the game was on the line, they kept fouling O'Neal because the odds that he'd miss were in their favor. Because of the widespread use of this tactic, only two other players in NBA history have gone to the line more than Shaq. He hired a coach to help him in this area and although he improved, his performance was still less than average. So what was the solution?

Keep Shaq off the line.

There may be some areas related to your business or career where you just need to "stay off the line." If you can delegate these activities to someone who is good at it, do it. It may cost you some money, but think about the time, energy, and frustration you'll save — not to mention avoiding mistakes that could have long-term implications.

Assemble a Realistic, Yet Aggressive Strategy

Depending on where a fighter is in his career, the training plan can look very different. For a newbie, training may address conditioning and fundamentals, where an experienced boxer preparing for a prize fight will likely focus on very specific areas of refinement.

One of the things I quickly realized in working with my private coaching clients is that everyone doesn't move at the same pace. What takes one person six months to accomplish may be completed in three weeks by another. When it comes to creating your strategy, resist the urge to compare your progress to someone else. The key is to keep pushing yourself out of your comfort zone and to stay committed to what you said you would accomplish, even if the timeline slips.

For every goal you set, make sure it's SMART: specific, measurable, attainable, relevant, and time-bound. By writing down exactly what you're going to do *by when*, you'll drastically improve your chances of accomplishing it.

Protect Yourself from Distractions

When a fighter is training for a title bout, they must go to great lengths to protect themselves from distractions that could undermine their progress. As you look to identify the distractions you need to eliminate, you may be thinking of common culprits like watching television or spending too much time online. But you may be surprised by the most dangerous sources of distraction in your life.

The medical definition for distraction is "diversion of the attention" — not "time wasters" or "futile activities." In this case, a distraction is anything that diverts your attention from fulfilling the purpose for which you were created.

Because you're good at what you do, people are always asking for your help. That could be at work, at church, in the community, and especially among your family and friends. Don't get me wrong. I'm not telling you to become completely selfish and refuse any requests to do anything that doesn't benefit you and the advancement of your professional life. But what *I am* saying is that if all the extra activities you're taking on are keeping you from completing your primary assignment, something has to change.

When your life comes to an end, do you want people to remember you as someone who was "always busy" or do you want to leave behind a legacy that will be felt for generations to come? People will soon forget that you missed a non-critical meeting or declined taking on an action item, but they'll always remember the impact that you made on the world by walking in your purpose.

Take inventory of everything that you have your hands in and if you don't have the time or energy to work on the efforts that will allow you to focus on your purpose, work on moving some of those activities off your plate.

Get a Good Coach

No matter how dedicated a boxer may be, he or she knows they will accomplish more with a good coach than they ever could alone.

I am a coach, but I'm wise enough to know that I still need a coach. I heard it best stated like this:

You can't see the picture if you are the frame.

To expect that you can figure out everything you need to do, do it, *and* objectively analyze what could be done to improve your results is an unfair expectation of yourself. As great as Michael Jordan was on the basketball court, he still knew that Coach Phil Jackson had valuable input from the sidelines that could help him win the game.

Different coaches have different styles, so do your homework to figure out what will work best for you. My approach tends to be a blend of coaching, consulting, and mentoring. Most people don't invest in a coach, because they're interested in a journey; they want results. I put on the right hat at the right time to help you get what you need.

Here are a few other considerations as you begin your work with a coach:

- **Find someone whose belief system lines up with yours**. If you have critical fundamental differences, it could impact your ability to work together.

- **Find a specialist**. If you can, look to work with a coach who specializes in solving the problem you have or who frequently works with people like you. A good coach can work with just about anyone and deliver results in multiple areas, but a specialist will likely be able to deliver faster, better results.

- **Recognize that your coach is not a mind reader.** Be honest about your challenges. Don't try to impress them with how smart or accomplished you are. Treat this as a confidante relationship in your Personal Advisory Board. Transparency and vulnerability will lead to better results.

- **Trust the process.** A good coach will often take time to get a firm understanding of who you are, what you really want to accomplish and how you operate before jumping to solutions. To do that, they may ask you questions or give you assignments that you don't see as relevant to what you're looking to accomplish. Be comfortable asking questions to help you understand, but keep yourself open to new approaches.

- **Stop telling yourself you can't afford it.** We find ways to invest in the things we care about. If you have to save up to work with a coach, do it.

A good coach can help you develop a winning strategy, push you to accomplish more than you ever could on your own, provide an objective voice, and "talk you off the ledge" when you're ready to give up. Deciding to hire my first coach in 2004 is the greatest investment I have ever made in my professional success and you wouldn't be holding this book in your hands if I hadn't (Thanks, Valorie!).

As you create and execute your training plan, be sure you're working on the right things at the right time. Don't invest thousands of dollars in expensive promotional materials for your business if you haven't even figured out how you're going to get paid. An amateur boxer may have his sights set on world championship bout in Vegas, but he'll never get there without committing to the grueling conditioning schedule today. Don't despise small beginnings. Your consistent efforts will yield a big payoff if you remain faithful to your plan.

> You can't see the picture if you are the frame.
>
> *- unknown*

Time for Action

Answer the questions below to assemble the framework for your Training Plan.

1. **Opponents I must defeat:**

2. **What I will do to get to the root of these challenges:**

3. **Deficiencies to address:**

4. **How I will improve in these areas, "stay off the line" or both?**

5. My SMART Goals (specific, measurable, attainable, relevant and time-bound):

6. Distractions to eliminate:

7. What will I do to get rid of them?

8. What I want to accomplish by working with a coach:

chapter 14

RULE No. 5: Don't Throw in the Towel

*Our greatest weakness lies in giving up. The most
certain way to succeed is always to try just one more time.*

Thomas A. Edison

Since his very first job out of college as a sales
representative in the telecommunications industry, Jaison
Ray knew he was wired for entrepreneurship.

"Even though I was an early stage employee, I was very
concerned with the bottom line. I looked at things as an
owner, albeit with none of the risk," Jaison said.

"I wanted to know what we were paying for office
space, what the phone bill was for a company that made the
volume of calls that we did. I wanted to know what portion
of the revenue we generated paid the bills and what was left
over.

After a nine-year stint in and out of telecom with a gig in senior management with a startup in between, Jaison landed his dream job with an investment banking firm. Until just like telecom, the bottom fell out of that industry, too.

Throughout his corporate career, Jaison always has had a business on the side — selling everything from water filters to cosmetics through multi-level marketing companies to launching a fledgling record label. He had varying degrees of success with these ventures until a barber shop visit planted a seed for what would become the heart of his entrepreneurial pursuits.

In 2002, Jaison launched his first concept-based clothing line. At the height of the company's success, the website was receiving 30,000 unique visits a month and was even featured in a fashion show hosted by a national cable network. But in the blink of an eye, the company no longer belonged to him.

So, what happened?

"In a word — apathy," Jaison stated. "In more than a word, I essentially trusted someone that I shouldn't have. We'll leave it right there."

But Jaison didn't throw in the towel.

"In the aftermath of finding out that my company had been taken from me — and that's exactly what happened — I was angry for about 90 minutes," he said. "That really still blows me away that I was only mad for an hour and a half when something I put roughly 10 years into was taken away from me, but that's what happened," he said.

"After I cooled down, the first statement that popped into my head was one that we've all said, or heard, or both: Everything happens for a reason. The answer to that question was what I needed. What's the reason? The reason was that there was something bigger and better in store for me. Because I was so blind when it came to the former line, I never really looked at it critically to see what I could do to make it better. With it getting taken away from me completely my mind was freed to receive something else."

Releasing the anger and refusing to become bitter proved to be a rewarding approach.

"The clothing line was taken from me on a Friday. That Sunday, I was hospitalized for four days. During that time, the foundation for what is now The I Am Apparel Group was born ... just like that," he shared.

In just a few short months, average monthly sales have already significantly outpaced the performance of his previous clothing line.

"The I Am Apparel Group empowers people to express themselves in a unique manner that they agree with, but may not have been able to come up with on their own," Jaison explains.

Each of the shirts in the initial line feature the words "I AM" followed by an acronym which is spelled out on the back. Some of the shirts include "I AM Gifted — God's Infinite Wisdom Transcends Every Detour" and for election season, "I AM A Voter – Voicing Our Thoughts Equally Respectfully."

Jaison is also creating unique partnerships with businesses to design signature shirts that align with their mission or brand. He recently formed a joint venture with an Ohio-based fitness company to form I AM Better Activewear, LLC. Together, the offshoot will produce a line of fitness-inspired T-shirts, training pants, and socks.

Over the past 18 years, Jaison has celebrated a number of wins in both his corporate and entrepreneurial endeavors, but he has certainly experienced his share of disappointments, too. More than once, he's had what he thought would be "the next big thing" in his hands, only to see it slip through his fingers. But no matter how many times he gets knocked down, Jaison keeps getting back up.

What's the most important characteristic for any fighter who wants to win? Endurance.

A typical boxing match lasts 12 rounds. In those 36 minutes, a fighter can throw upwards of 800 punches and land fewer than 25 percent. Sounds like lots of effort with little impact, doesn't it? But all it takes is one punch to knock out the opponent.

When it comes to your professional life, you don't know where your knockout punch will come from, which project will be the ticket to the role you've been dreaming of, or which connection will lead to a seven-figure business opportunity.

Feel like you've been taking a lot of hits? A fighter can withstand hundreds of blows in those 12 rounds and still manage to emerge victoriously. No matter how bad you're getting beat up at work or in your business, don't assume you've lost the fight.

Whether you end up on the winning side of the equation is largely a matter of endurance. If you don't remember anything else from this chapter, remember this: ***You won't win if you stop fighting.***

"There's a question that is often asked in sales," Jaison said. "If you knew that at the end of 10 years you would have earned 10 million dollars, would you quit?" Of course not! But here's the thing, you're not guaranteed to earn 1 million dollars a year every year. You might get 3 million in year five and nothing else for another five years. But if you knew what was coming, you wouldn't give up."

"You don't have to assign a dollar amount to it — it's whatever goal you're ultimately after," He urges. "Begin with that in mind and act accordingly."

You may need to lie on the ropes for a minute to regain your composure. If you get knocked down, don't stay there too long, or you may get counted out. And most important:

Don't ever throw in the towel.

As Jaison reflects over the ups and downs of his professional life, he offers this advice, "You can't lose if you don't give up. Period."

Time for Action

What is the ultimate goal that you want to accomplish?

Why is accomplishing this goal so important to you?

How will others benefit when you are successful?

What will you do to stay motivated when you want to throw in the towel?

It's Time to Get in the Ring

Understand that when you step into the ring, there's a 50 percent chance that you'll win and a 50 percent chance that you'll lose. Is your vision worth accepting the odds and getting in the ring anyway?

Every effort may not be successful. I'm not sure where we ever got the impression that it would be. Just like a scientist in the lab, analyze the data and figure out what went wrong and make the necessary adjustments until you get the outcome you're looking for.

Along the way, what you want may change or you may decide that you're not willing to invest the effort necessary to achieve your original goals. Certain opportunities may vanish for good. But before resigning yourself to believing it is over, ask yourself, "Is there another way I still can accomplish my original purpose?"

When I was 14, I decided that I wanted to be a television reporter. I've always been a bit of a ham, so being on camera everyday seemed like a good fit. But there were two aspects that appealed to me more than anything.

First, I enjoyed meeting new people and learning interesting things about them. I remember watching Donnie Simpson, host of the 90s cable show, Video Soul, interview all of my favorite entertainers and feeling like he had the best job in the world!

Second, I wanted my work to inspire people to do great things. I remember hearing famed motivational speaker Les Brown when I was 9 years old. He made me feel something I had never felt before, and I knew then that I wanted to make people feel the same way. Over the next few years, I saw more and more speakers and they all seemed to have either overcome some tremendous challenge or have done something really awesome. At 14, I didn't fit either of those descriptions, so to be a speaker that someone would listen to, I thought being a recognized personality from television news would give me enough credibility to get people to listen to me.

By the time I got ready to graduate from college with a degree in broadcast journalism, I realized I didn't enjoy news. I liked to make people feel good, but it seemed that everything that came out of our mouths was doom and gloom. When I pursued my "back-up career" in public relations, I had completely forgotten why I really was interested in becoming a reporter in the first place.

When I look at my career today, I am doing exactly what I set out to do at 14. Through my speaking and coaching, I get to meet new people and learn interesting things about them, and I'm also blessed with the gift of being able to inspire people to do great things. The past two decades of life have also presented opportunities to overcome tremendous challenges and do some pretty awesome things like those speakers I had heard during my childhood. And I haven't completely gotten away from television either. I've had numerous opportunities to make appearances both as a host and guest, and we're planning the launch of an online show soon.

Your career may take any number of twists and turns, but don't lose sight of your purpose. What is it that you were put on this earth to accomplish? There may be dozens of different ways that you can fulfill that purpose. Be open to success showing up looking differently than you originally planned. The important thing is that you fulfill your assignment.

When you live everyday with your purpose in mind, you'll be amazed at how much you can tolerate without being shaken. In the words of my favorite scripture,

Romans 8:28, you'll realize that all things will work together for your good when you love God and are called according to His purpose.

The fight is fixed, my friend. You can't lose!

Acknowledgements

There are so many people who have played a critical role in this book being in your hands.

To my parents, A. Whitney Cogborn and Gloria Kling, you always made me feel like I could do anything. I still believe it.

To my son, Deon, you are the absolute sunshine of my life. Can't wait to see what God has in store for your life.

To my editor and friend, La Toya Rosario and her husband, Luis, thank you for saving the day! I'm looking forward to handing off the complete publishing project on the next one. Your gifts will bring you before great men.

To Kim and Jarod, words cannot express what your friendship means to me, so I won't even try.

To my all of my family, Cogborn, Holland, Cook, Harris, and Crayton, our latter shall be greater. Granny, I love you.

To the ...*But I Don't Want a REAL Job!* community — especially Kendra Tillman — thank you for inspiring me. You remind me every day why I exist.

To my spiritual parents, Sean R. and Erica R. Moore, thank you for pushing me to be yattir. I'm so grateful to you and the entire Faith Christian Center family.

And to all of my clients, past, present and future, in the words of Brian Adams, "Everything I do, I do it for you."

Thank You, Lord, for giving me such an awesome assignment on this side of heaven. You didn't let me stray too far from my purpose and still worked it out for my good when I did. My answer is still yes.

Coach Isha Speaks!

Schedule Coach Isha's passionate and practical workshops to unleash the **potential, purpose,** and **power** in your people!

If you're looking for a dynamic program for your group that won't only entertain, but deliver life-changing impact for your audience, Isha Cogborn is your answer. Her energetic presence, engaging style, and practical, no-nonsense advice make her a favorite from the boardroom to the dorm room.

Isha provides training, keynote addresses and facilitation for both professional and student audiences and can create customized programming to meet your group's unique needs.

To inquire about bringing Isha to your organization or event, send an email to Info@CoachIsha.com or request more information online at www.CoachIsha.com.

A Final Thought from Coach Isha

Has this book made a difference in your life? I want to hear from you! Send me an email at info@CoachIsha.com. I personally read and make an effort to respond to every message. I may even ask to feature you in an upcoming article, media segment or even my next book.

Join the Movement

We're on a mission to get this book in the hands of one million people around the world. Sound crazy? Not with your help. Think of how different society will be when one million people ditch fear and paralysis and use their talents, abilities, passions and experiences to solve the world's problems.

If you know someone who could benefit from this book, tell them about it. Even better, consider giving a copy as a gift.

Work doesn't have to be a four-letter word. Let's join forces to change the world.

Time for Action

Who do you know that needs a copy of this book?

Made in the USA
Columbia, SC
19 August 2024

40259775R00072